Advent Calendar Coloring Paper Craft. Make your own Advent Calendar with Quotes

If you'd like to see a video of how the book is assembled, here's my Youtube channel. Scan the code and it will take you directly to the video! Thank you!

You could also search for the video on Youtube with the keyword "Pixieishcreations Advent Calendar".

Advent Calendar
Coloring Paper Craft

Make your Own
Advent Calendar
with Quotes

How to assemble the Advent Calendar

The paper craft project consists of 4 parts that should be individually assembled and the glued to form a book. I suggest coloring the parts first, then glueing the window parts to cover the quotes and only afterwards to assemble each part. Each window/door has a number that matches the numbers on the wall base page and they should be matched before glued.

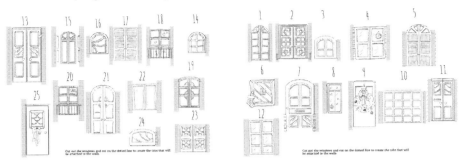

Fold the parts marked with grey and glue them to the walls base page

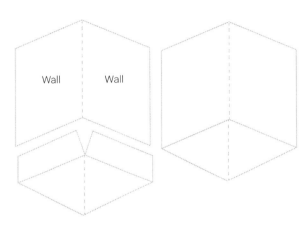

Now you can glue the extra items. Fold the paper strips into square shaped parts that you will use to glue the extra elements to the base paper.

Final step

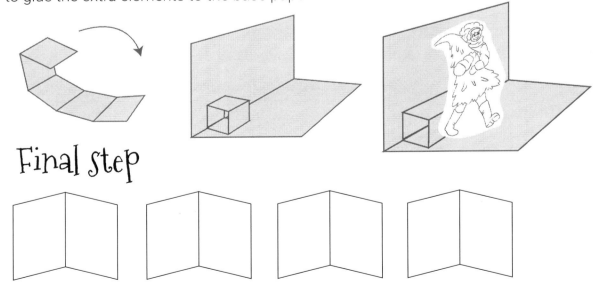

Fold all the parts in the center so that they all open and glue the 4 parts together. Glue the cover on top.

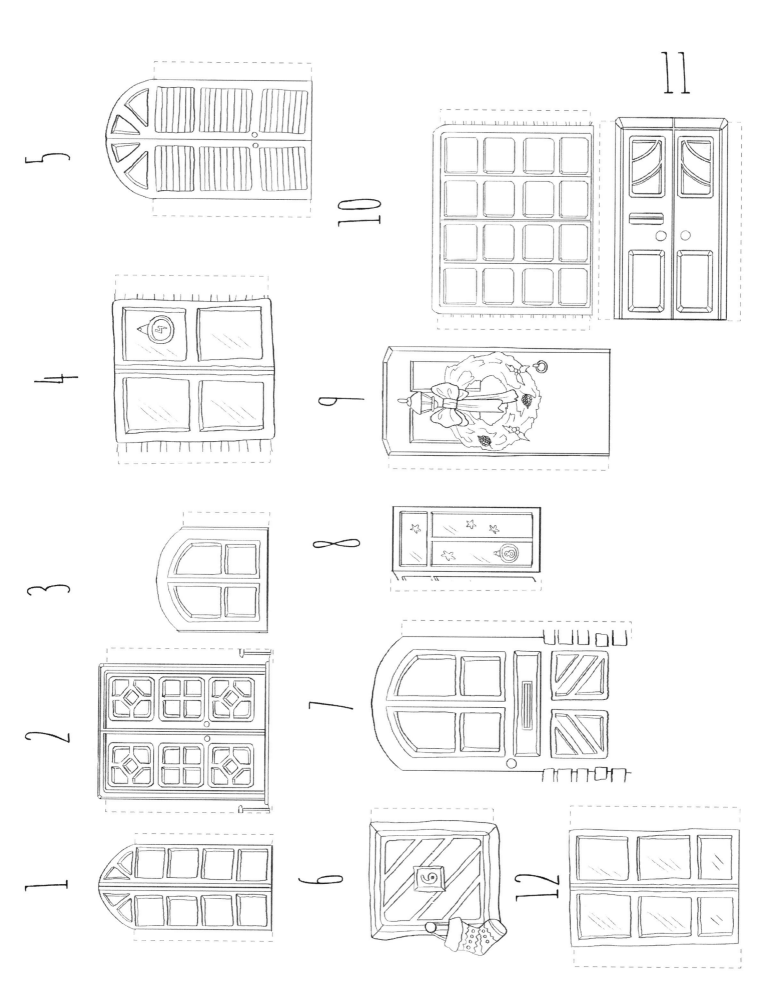

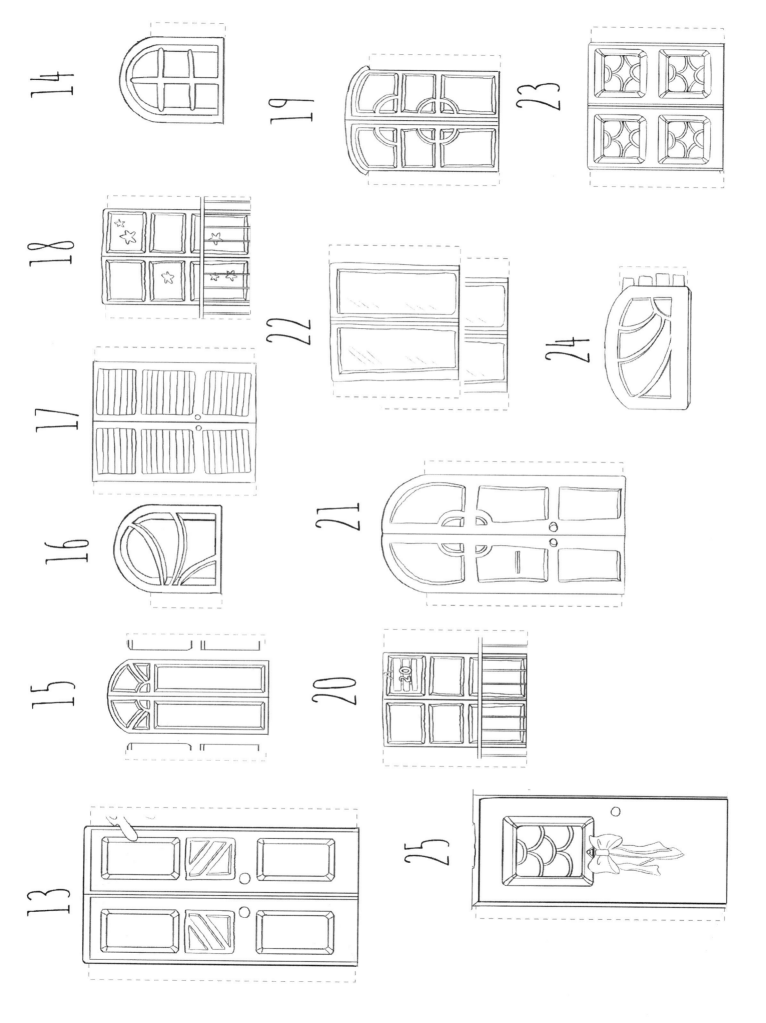

14

19

23

18

22

24

17

16

21

15

20

13

25

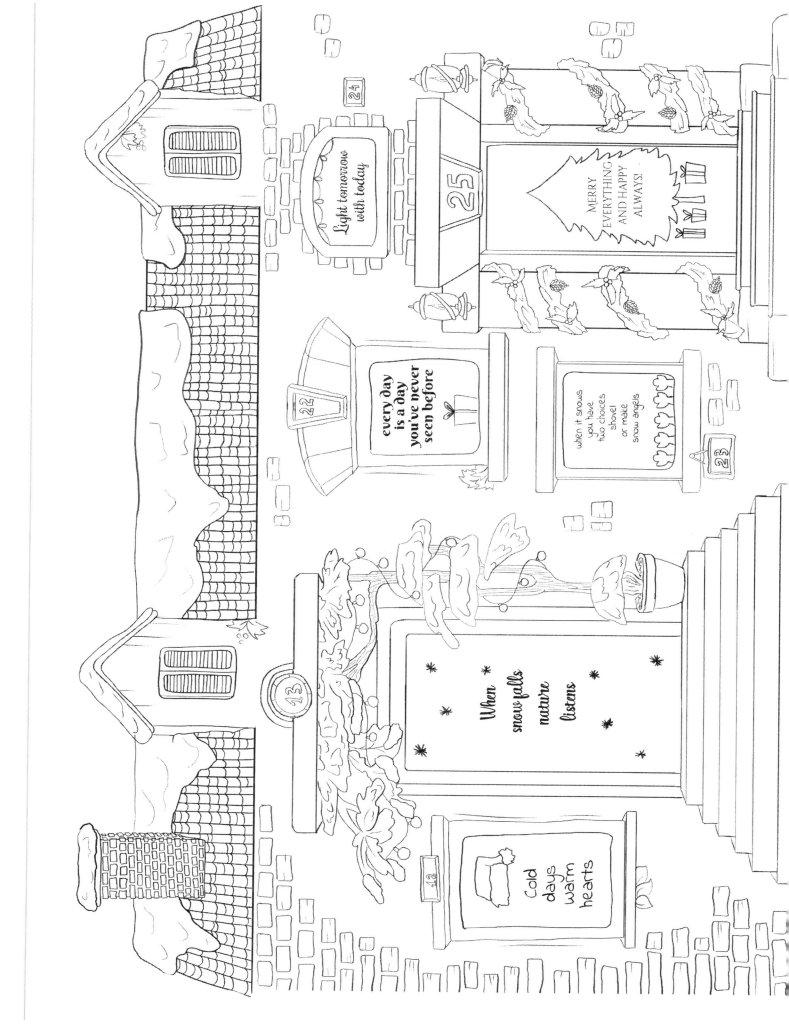

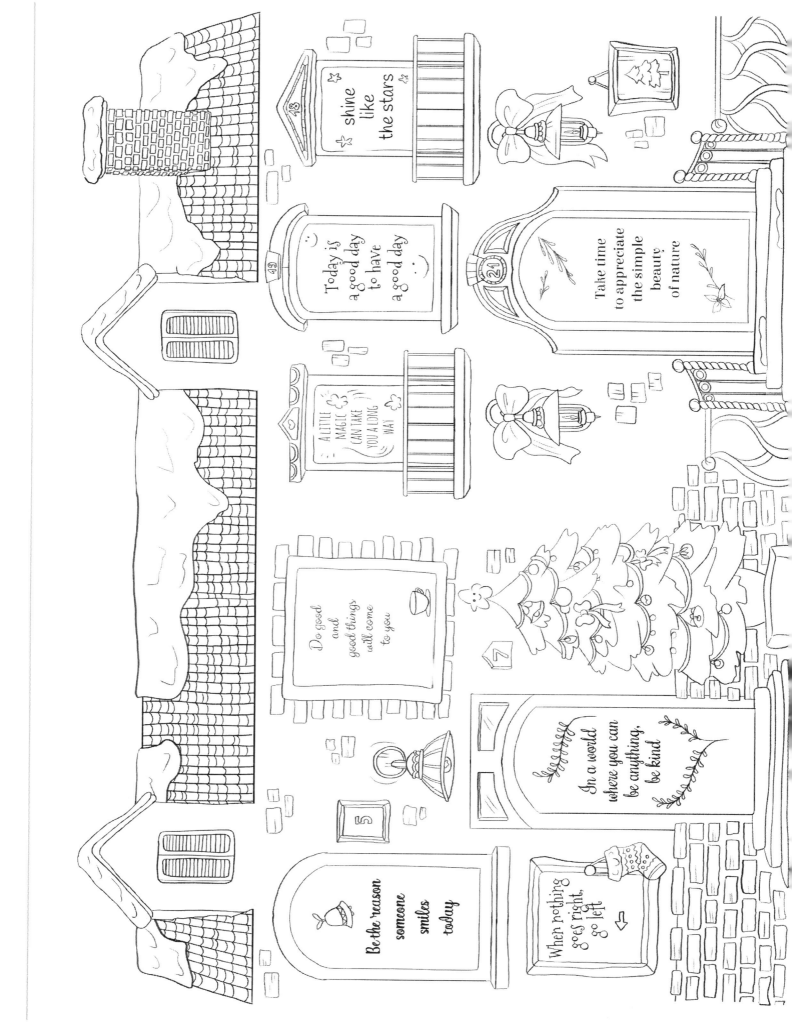

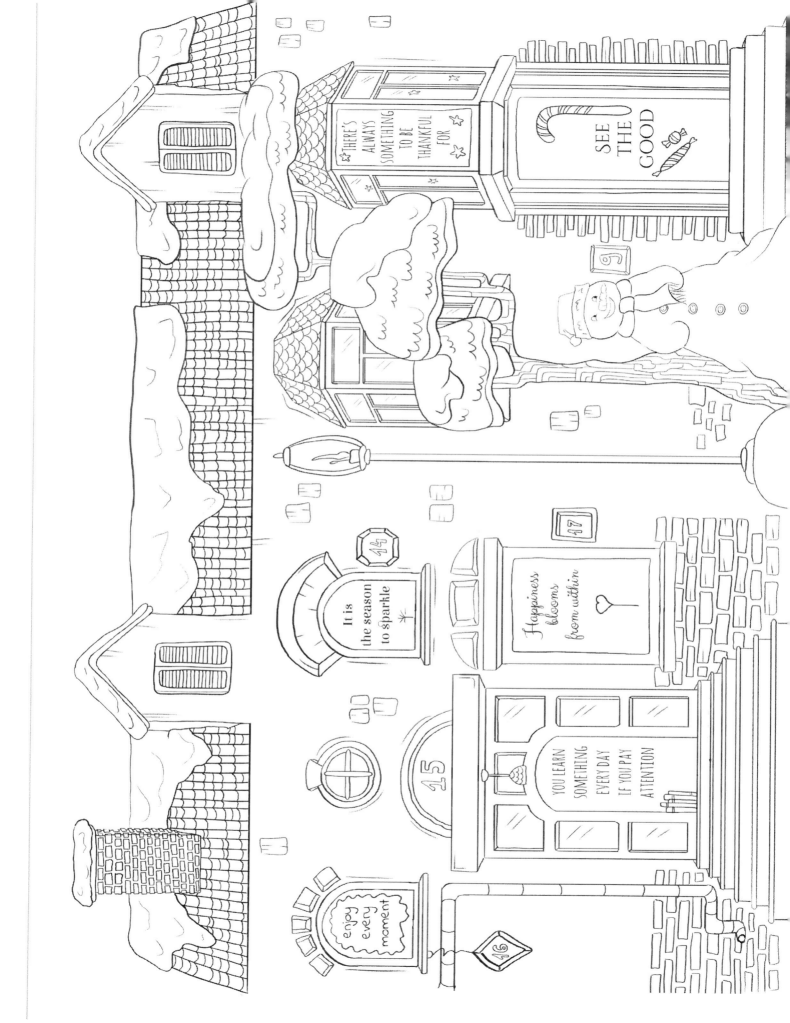

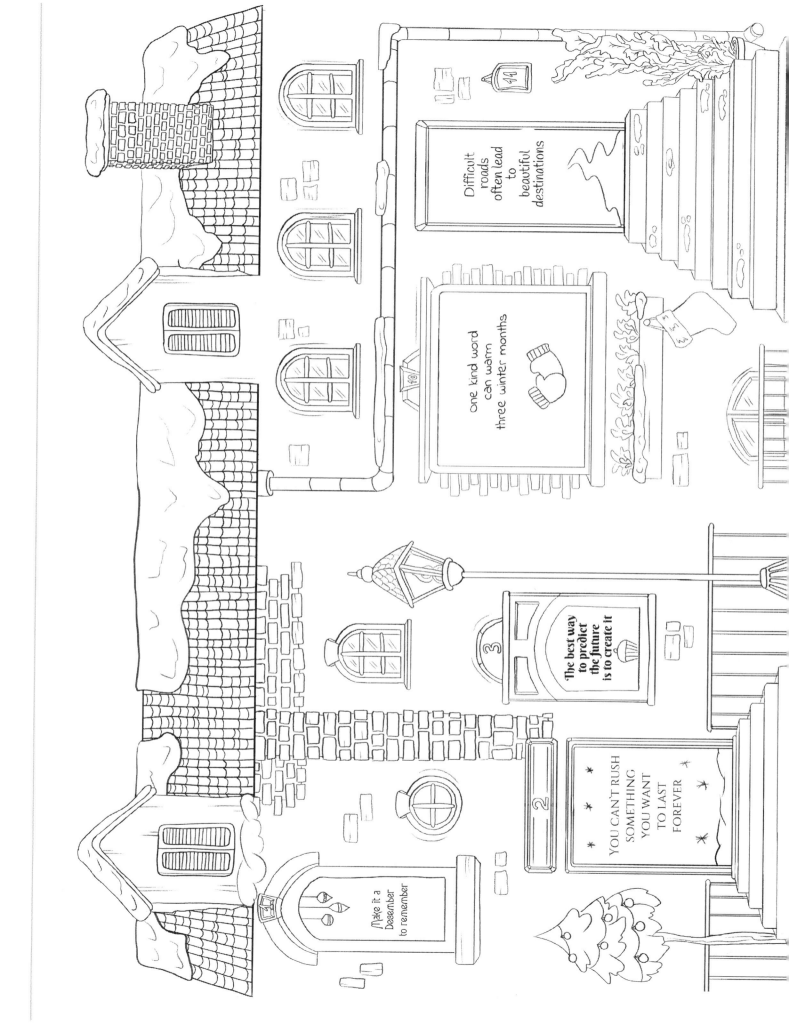

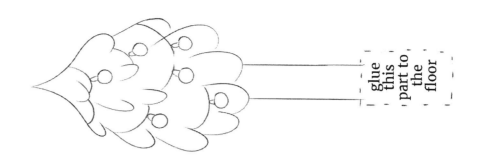

glue
this
part to
the
floor

glue this
part to
the wall

glue this
part to
the tree

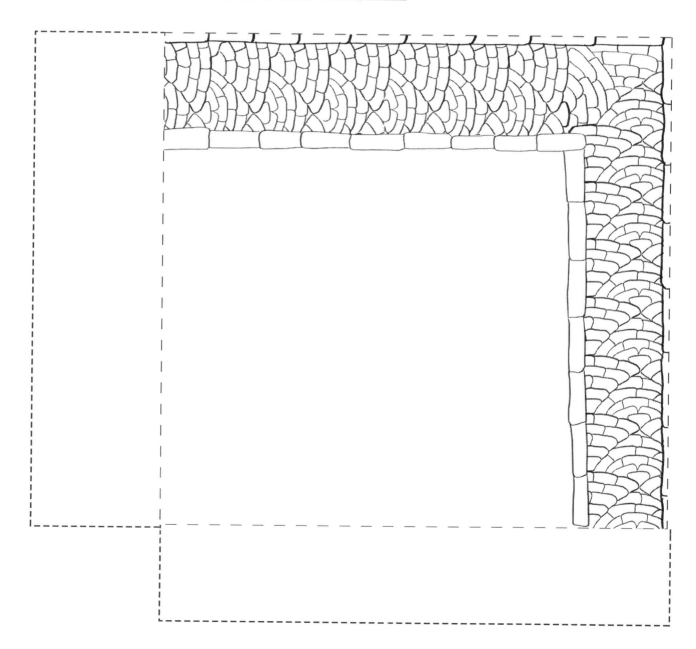

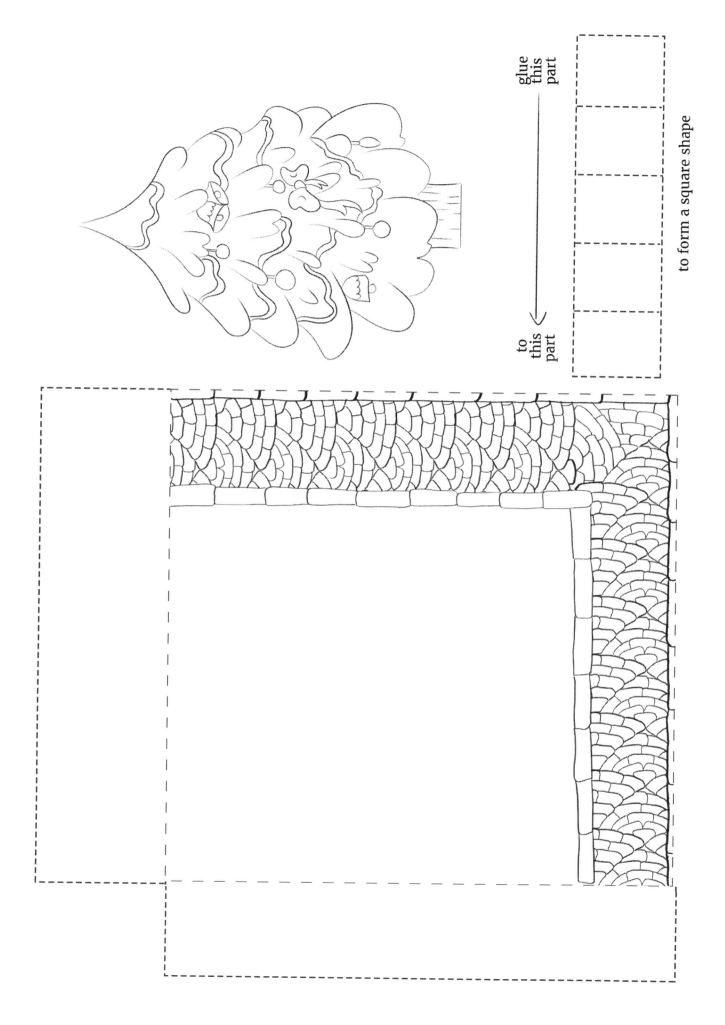

glue this part

to this part

to form a square shape

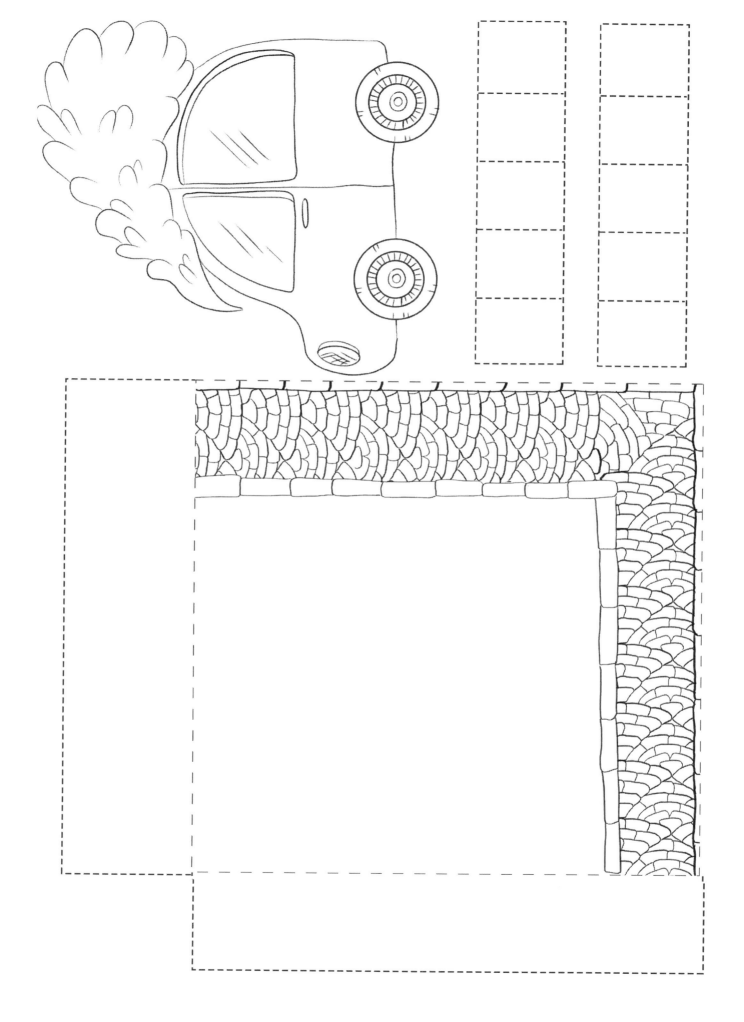

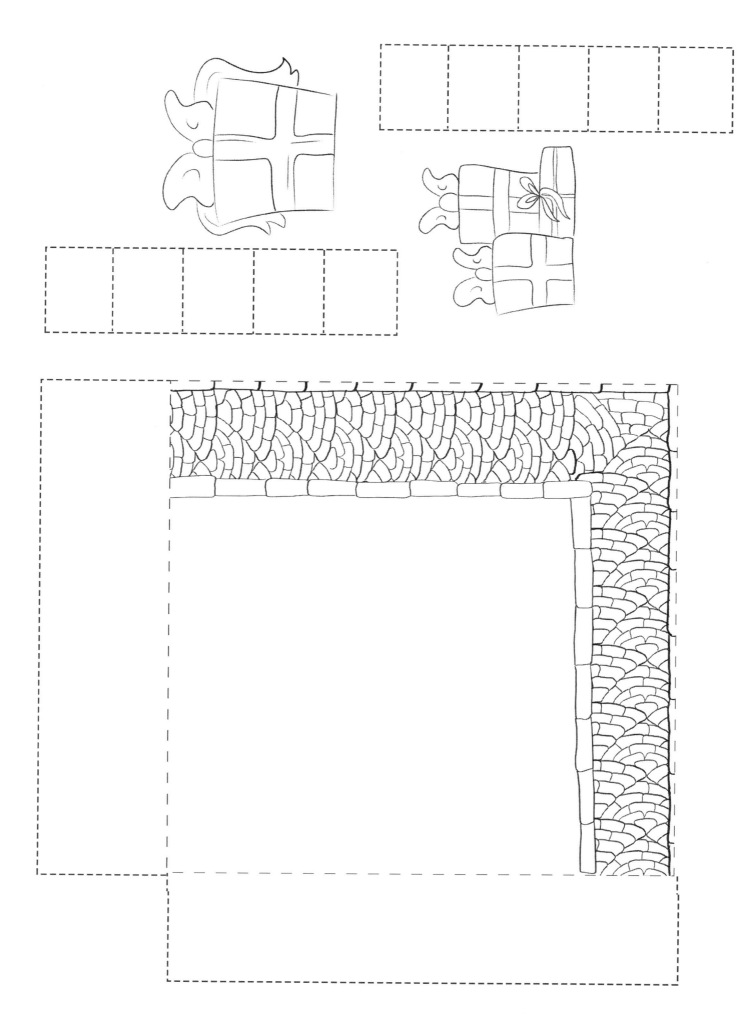

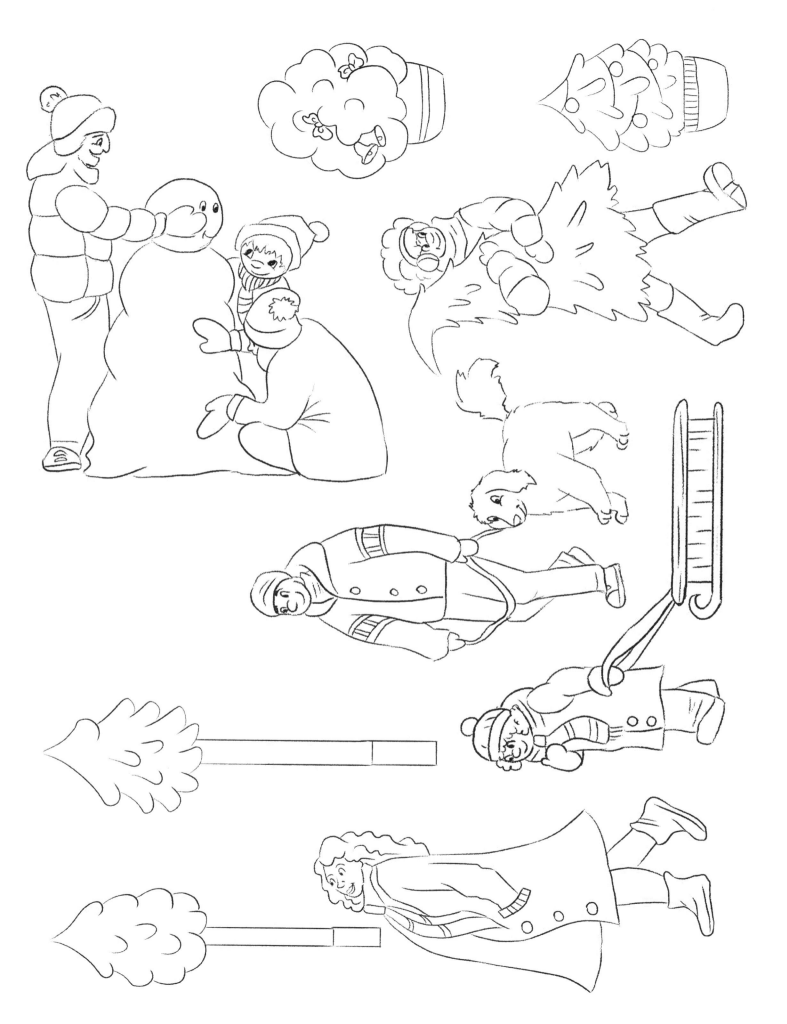

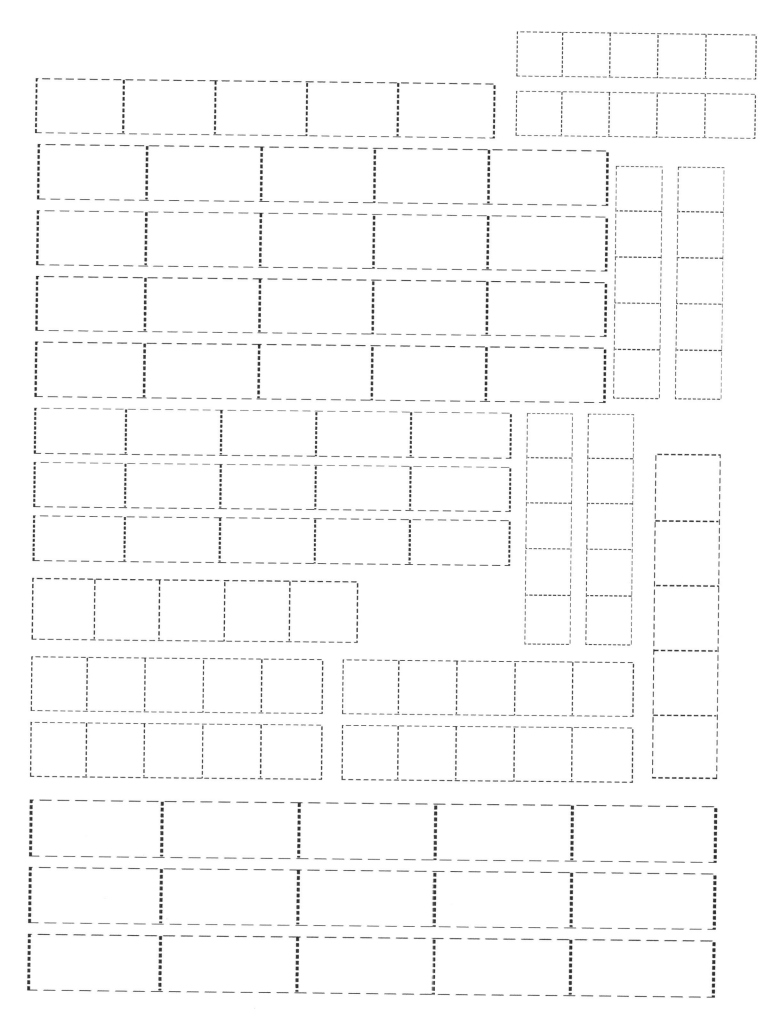

Made in the USA
Monee, IL
01 October 2023

43761628R00017